# TEXTS AND STUDIES

## CONTRIBUTIONS TO
## BIBLICAL AND PATRISTIC LITERATURE

EDITED BY

## J. ARMITAGE ROBINSON D.D.

HON. PH.D. GÖTTINGEN    HON. D.D. HALLE
NORRISIAN PROFESSOR OF DIVINITY

VOL. V

## No. 3.   THE HYMN OF THE SOUL.

# THE HYMN OF THE SOUL

CONTAINED IN

# THE SYRIAC ACTS OF ST THOMAS

RE-EDITED

WITH AN ENGLISH TRANSLATION

BY

## ANTHONY ASHLEY BEVAN M.A

FELLOW OF TRINITY COLLEGE CAMBRIDGE
LORD ALMONER'S READER IN ARABIC

*Wipf & Stock*
PUBLISHERS
*Eugene, Oregon*

Man höret oft im fernen Wald
Von obenher ein dumpfes Läuten,
Doch niemand weiss, von wann es hallt,
Und kaum die Sage kann es deuten.
Von der verlornen Kirche soll
Der Klang ertönen mit den Winden;
Einst war der Pfad von Wallern voll,
Nun weiss ihn keiner mehr zu finden.

LUDWIG UHLAND.

Wipf and Stock Publishers
199 W 8th Ave, Suite 3
Eugene, OR 97401

The Hymn of the Soul
contained in Syriac Acts of St. Thomas
By Bevan, Anthony Ashley
ISBN: 1-59244-831-3
Publication date 8/26/2004
Previously published by Cambridge, 1897

# PREFACE.

THE Poem which forms the subject of this monograph was first published and translated by the late William Wright, Professor of Arabic in the University of Cambridge, in his *Apocryphal Acts of the Apostles* (2 vols. London, 1871). Since then the Syriac text has been re-edited in the third volume of the *Acta Martyrum et Sanctorum* (Paris, 1892), and two German translations, with copious explanatory remarks, have appeared—that of Karl Macke in the *Theologische Quartalschrift* (Tübingen) for 1874, pp. 3—70, and that of Lipsius in his work *Die apokryphen Apostelgeschichten und Apostellegenden* vol. i. (Brunswick, 1883) pp. 292—300, vol. ii. pt. ii. (1884) p. 422.

As Prof. Wright's book has for several years been out of print, it seemed all the more desirable to re-publish the poem in a convenient form. If the piece were an integral part of the Apocryphal Acts, there might be some objection to thus detaching it from the context in which it stands; but, as a matter of fact, it is an independent composition and may therefore be treated separately. When we consider its antiquity and its highly original character, it must appear extraordinary that it should hitherto have attracted so little attention among theologians; if I succeed in exciting any further interest in this master-piece of religious poetry, the main object of my work will have been attained. At the same time I venture to hope that I have been able to contribute something fresh towards the elucidation of the text, in particular towards the comprehension of the metre, which is necessarily of great importance in textual criticism. Since the first editor, Prof. Wright, is universally acknowledged to have been one of the highest authorities in the department of Syriac literature, it may seem presumptuous, in a pupil of his, to think of supplementing, or modifying, the conclusions at which he arrived. I may therefore be allowed to state explicitly that the

1 *

cases in which my interpretation differs from Prof. Wright's are few indeed as compared with those in which I have found his guidance invaluable. The first translator of so singular a document, however learned and however careful he may be, can scarcely hope to produce a perfect version, and Prof. Wright, as may be seen from his notes, was far from making such a claim. If I have ventured to explain some passages in a different manner, this has been chiefly in consequence of the fact that I was able to avail myself of various suggestions offered by other scholars who, during the last twenty-six years, have made a special study of the text. The most important of these contributions are due to Prof. Nöldeke; some of them appeared in his review of Prof. Wright's book (*Zeitschrift der deutschen morgenländischen Gesellschaft* for 1871, pp. 670—679), others he privately communicated to Lipsius, in whose work (mentioned above) they are cited, others again I have received from him directly, either by word of mouth or in writing, together with his permission to publish them. For this great kindness I beg here to offer him my sincerest thanks. At the same time I desire to express my gratitude to the Editor of this Series, Prof. J. Armitage Robinson, for several suggestions which I have gladly adopted.

In order to insure the accuracy of the text I have, of course, examined for myself the MS in the British Museum. The only mistake worth mentioning which I have been able to detect in Prof. Wright's edition, occurs in verse 71 *a*; here Prof. Wright's *conjecture* is really the reading of the MS.

It need hardly be said that in the *Introduction* I have not attempted to give anything like a systematic analysis of the poet's theology, but have confined myself to indicating some of its more important features. The character of my work being mainly philological, I must leave the task of historical exposition to be completed by persons who possess a very much wider knowledge of the science of comparative religion.

A. A. BEVAN.

TRINITY COLLEGE,
*Nov.* 1897.

# CONTENTS.

|                        |      | PAGE |
| ---------------------- | ---- | ---- |
| INTRODUCTION           |  .   |  1   |
| TEXT AND TRANSLATION   |  .   |  9   |
| NOTES                  |  .   |  32  |

# INTRODUCTION

THE text here edited is based upon a single manuscript, Brit. Mus. Add. 14645, bearing the date A. Gr. 1247 (= A.D. 936) and containing a collection of Lives of Saints. For a full description, see Wright's *Catalogue of the Syriac Manuscripts in the British Museum*, No. DCCCCLII (pp. 1111—1116). Foremost in the collection are placed the Acts of St Thomas, or, as the Syriac heading calls them, "The Acts of Judas Thomas the Apostle," which occupy 49 leaves. The Poem begins on fol. 30 *b*, and is introduced in the following manner. The Apostle, we are told, in the course of his journeys through India, was arrested and cast into prison by order of a king named Mazdai. In the prison he offers up a prayer, at the conclusion of which we read—"*And whilst he was praying, all those who were in the prison saw that he was praying and begged of him to pray for them too. And when he had prayed and sat down, Judas began to chant this hymn. The Hymn of Judas Thomas the Apostle in the country of the Indians.*" Here follows the Poem, with the subscription—"*The Hymn of Judas Thomas the Apostle, which he spake in the prison, is ended.*" But the Poem itself contains not the remotest allusion to the circumstances described in the preceding narrative, nor is there anything in the remainder of the narrative to indicate that the narrator was acquainted with the Poem. The question therefore arises, Was the Poem composed by the author of the Acts or was it derived from some other source?

This is not the place to discuss the origin and history of the Acts of St Thomas, for which the reader may refer to Lipsius, *Die apokryphen Apostelgeschichten und Apostellegenden* vol. i. pp. 225—347, vol. ii. pt. ii. pp. 423—425, and to Harnack, *Die*

*Chronologie der altchristlichen Litteratur bis Eusebius* vol. i.
(Leipsic, 1897) pp. 545—549. Here it is enough to say that
these Acts are extant both in Syriac and in Greek[1], but it is still
disputed in which language they were originally composed. In
the Greek Acts of St Thomas the Poem with which we are con-
cerned is absent, nor is any trace of it to be found in the Berlin
MS of the Syriac text (Sachau Collection, No. 222)—see the *Acta
Martyrum et Sanctorum* vol. iii. (Paris, 1892) p. 110 note[2]. Hence
the controversy as to the original language of the Acts does not
in any way affect the Poem, for even those who believe the Acts
to have been first composed in Greek admit that the Poem is not
a translation but a purely Syriac work. This, as Nöldeke pointed
out in 1871, is evident from the style and, in particular, from the
metrical character of the piece. In these respects it differs greatly
from the other hymns and prayers which the Acts contain. Both
external and internal evidence therefore lead us to the conclusion
that the Poem was borrowed from some extraneous source and
inserted—at what period we cannot say—into the Acts. Happily
it is not of any great importance to decide how it found its way
into this context; the question which interests us is how it
originated. We are here entirely dependent on internal evidence; for, as every Syriac scholar must see at once that the piece
is much older than the 10th century, the date affixed to the MS
tells us nothing which we might not have safely assumed.

The considerations of which we have to take account, in con-
ducting this inquiry, may be briefly summed up as follows.
Obscure as many passages undoubtedly are, the general drift of
the Poem is quite clear, and cannot be better described than in the
words of Nöldeke—"We have here an ancient Gnostic hymn
relating to the Soul, which is sent from its heavenly home to the
earth[3], and there forgets both its origin and its mission until it is

---

[1] Edited by Max Bonnet, *Acta Thomae* (Leipsic, 1883).

[2] My friend Mr F. C. Burkitt informs me that after a very careful search he
was unable to discover any part of the Poem among the fragments of the Syriac
Acts of St Thomas in the Library of the Convent on Mount Sinai.

[3] The choice of "Egypt" as the type of this world, the abode of evil and
particularly of "slavery" (couplet 44), is no doubt *ultimately* based upon the Old
Testament. Nöldeke points out that a similar metaphorical use of "Egypt" is

aroused by a revelation from on high ; thereupon it performs the task assigned to it and returns to the upper regions, where it is reunited to the heavenly robe, its ideal counterpart, and enters the presence of the highest celestial Powers." But if the general Gnostic character of the Poem seems evident, the precise nature of the Gnosticism, the date and the authorship are by no means so easy to determine. The difficulty of answering these questions is due mainly to the extreme meagreness of our information respecting the history of Syriac literature at the period when Gnosticism flourished, namely from the 2nd century to the beginning of the 4th. Though there is clear proof that Gnosticism exercised a powerful influence in Syria at that time, not only have the writings of the Syrian Gnostics almost entirely perished—which was merely what we might have expected—but the writings of their orthodox opponents have, with few and small exceptions, perished likewise. The ages of Justin Martyr, of Irenaeus, and of Origen are practically a blank in Syriac literature ; the oldest Syriac writer of whom we possess any considerable remains is Aphraates, in the first half of the 4th century[1]. Thus the problem before us is one which does not admit of anything like a final solution. Yet there are not wanting indications which, though uncertain if considered separately, may enable us at least to form a plausible hypothesis.

Of the Gnostic sects which existed in the Syriac-speaking lands by far the most important were the Bardesanists and the Manichaeans[2]. These two schools had, it is true, some features in

ascribed to the Naasseni and the Peratae—see Hippolytus, *The Refutation of All Heresies* Bk. v. chaps. 2 and 11.

[1] In the discussions which have lately taken place respecting the origin of the Pĕshîttâ version, this important fact seems to me to have been too frequently overlooked. Where scarcely any evidence exists, it is futile to bring forward " arguments from silence."

[2] On Bardesanes, see Merx, *Bardesanes von Edessa* (Halle, 1863) and Hort, Art. " Bardaisan " in the *Dictionary of Christian Biography* vol. i. (1877). Perhaps the best general account of Manichaeism is that by Spiegel in his *Erânische Alterthumskunde* vol. ii. (Leipsic, 1873) pp. 195—232 ; Kessler's *Mani* (Berlin, 1889) contains much valuable material on the subject, but should be used with great caution —see the review by Nöldeke in the *Zeitschrift der deutschen morgenländischen Gesellschaft* for 1889, pp. 535—549, and the note in the same periodical for 1890, p. 899.

common, for which reason Ephraim Syrus speaks of Bardesanes as
"the teacher of Mānī"[1]; but they nevertheless differed profoundly,
and, if we may trust the testimony of the Arabic writer An-Nadīm,
the founder of Manichaeism himself published refutations of the
Bardesanists[2]. It is therefore natural, in the case of a Gnostic
document composed in Syriac, to begin by inquiring whether
it can, with any probability, be ascribed to either of these sects.

That this Poem is not a Manichaean product hardly needs to
be stated. The most prominent idea in it, namely that the Soul
is "sent" from heaven to earth in order to perform a divine
mission, is quite contrary to the principles of Manichaeism; for
according to the Manichaean view the conjunction of the soul with
the body is the result of a "mixture" of the elements of Light and
of Darkness, which took place before the world was fashioned[3].

Of the religious teaching of Bardesanes (A.D. 154—222) very
little can be known with certainty. His writings have all been
lost, and the celebrated Dialogue on Fate[4] (or "the Book of the
Laws of the Countries"), which was composed by his disciple
Philip[5], is mainly devoted to proving the theory of human free-
will, to the almost total exclusion of religion properly so called.
So scanty is the evidence on this subject that in recent years some
have even doubted whether Bardesanes can rightly be described
as a Gnostic[6]. But though we have no trustworthy account of his

---

[1] ܠܒ̈ܢܘܗܝ ܪܒܐ ܗܘ ܡܢܝ ܐܬܟܪܙ *S. Ephraemi Syri .... Opera
selecta*, ed. Overbeck (Oxford, 1865) p. 63.

[2] G. Flügel, *Mani* (Leipsic, 1862) pp. 73, 102, where Mānī's "refutation of the
Daiṣānites (i.e. Bardesanists) on the subject of the Soul of Life" is mentioned.

[3] It may however be worth while to point out that the passage in which the
victory of the soul over the power of evil is symbolised by the prince "charming"
the serpent to sleep (couplets 58, 59) bears a curious resemblance to the Manichaean
myth described by Titus of Bostra (ed. De Lagarde, Bk. i. chap. 17)—Θεασαμένη γὰρ
ἡ ὕλη τὴν ἀποσταλεῖσαν δύναμιν, προσεκίσσησε μὲν ὡς ἐρασθεῖσα, ὁρμῇ δὲ πλείονι λαβοῦσα
ταύτην κατέπιε καὶ ἐδέθη τρόπον τινὰ ὥσπερ θηρίον. κέχρηνται γὰρ καὶ τῷδε τῷ ὑπο-
δείγματι, ὡς δι' ἐπῳδῆς τῆς ἀποσταλείσης δυνάμεως ἐκοιμίσθη. Instead of "the Hylē,"
the parallel passage in the *Fihrist* of An-Nadīm (G. Flügel, *Mani* pp. 54, 87) has
"the Primal Devil," which is doubtless a more faithful representation of the
Manichaean idea.

[4] Edited by Cureton in his *Spicilegium Syriacum* (London, 1855).

[5] See Wright, *A Short History of Syriac Literature* (London, 1894) p. 30.

[6] See F. Nau, *Une Biographie inédite de Bardesane l'Astrologue* (Paris, 1897).

theological system as a whole, it is impossible to deny, first, that he was regarded by the orthodox as a dangerous heretic, and, secondly, that some at least of the heresies ascribed to him are such as other Gnostics are known to have taught. Thus our principal authority on the question, Ephraim Syrus[1], who lived about a century and a half after Bardesanes, writes—"The woe which our Lord uttered came upon Bardaiṣān, who taught that there are Seven Essences (îthyê), and whom the iron of truth cut off and left to himself"[2]. These last words imply that Bardesanes was, if not formally excommunicated by the ecclesiastical authorities, at least considered as one outside the pale of the orthodox Church. Ephraim's accusations against Bardesanes fall under three principal heads—(1) that he denied the resurrection and regarded the separation of the soul from the body as a blessing[3], (2) that he held the theory of a divine "Mother" who in conjunction with "the Father of Life" gave birth to a being called "the Son of the Living"[4], (3) that he believed in a number of lesser "gods," that is to say, eternal beings subordinate to the supreme God[5].

Now it is remarkable that these three "heresies" all appear distinctly in the Poem before us. There can be no doubt that the Egyptian garb, which the prince puts on as a disguise and casts away as soon as his mission is accomplished, represents the human body. The emphatic declaration that the "filthy and unclean garb" is "left in their country" conveys an unmistakable meaning; it would be difficult, in an allegorical piece, to deny a material resurrection more absolutely. The true clothing of the soul, according to the poet, is the ideal form which it left behind in heaven and will reassume after death. As for the Father of Life

---

[1] To the usual references in the writings of Ephraim add *Comm. in Epp. Pauli* (on the apocryphal Third Epistle to the Corinthians), Armenian version, Venice 1836, translated into Latin by the Mechitarists, Venice 1893; a translation of this section, by Prof. Hübschmann, is given in Zahn's *Geschichte des neutestamentlichen Kanons*, 1890, vol. ii. pp. 595 *seq.*

[2] *S. Ephraemi Syri Opera omnia* (Roman ed.) vol. ii. p. 550.

[3] This is the accusation most frequently and most vehemently urged—see *S. Ephraemi Syri Carmina Nisibena*, ed. Bickell (Leipsic, 1866), hymns xlvi and li.

[4] Roman ed. vol. ii. p. 557. Whether Hort be right in identifying the "Mother" with the Holy Ghost, who, in the passage immediately following, is represented as giving birth to two daughters, I do not venture to determine.

[5] *Ibid.* pp. 443, 554, 558.

the Mother, and the Son of the Living, they here figure as the Father "the King of kings," the Mother "the Queen of the East," and the Brother "the next in rank." Finally the "lesser gods" appear as the "kings" (couplet 38), who obey the command of the King of kings. In addition to these ideas we here find others which are not expressly ascribed to Bardesanes but are nevertheless perfectly consistent with what we know of him. Thus the Platonic doctrine of reminiscence (ἀνάμνησις), which is expressed with such distinctness in the Poem (couplets 11, 55—57), can hardly have been unknown to Bardesanes, who, according to Epiphanius, was skilled in Greek as well as in Syriac[1]; moreover the Dialogue written by a disciple of Bardesanes, to which I have already referred, is so obviously modelled on the Platonic dialogues as to imply that the works of Plato were read in the circle to which the author belonged.

The foregoing considerations do not indeed suffice to prove that this Poem is a Bardesanist work, but they render it at least highly probable. Whether we have any reason to believe that it was composed by Bardesanes himself—as Nöldeke suggested, with some hesitation, in the year 1871—is a much more difficult question. Ephraim Syrus (Roman ed. vol. ii. pp. 553, 554) speaks of the hymns (madhrāshē) of Bardesanes, and mentions, in particular, a collection of 150 songs (zĕmīrāthā), after the number of the pieces in the Psalter. In another homily (ibid. pp. 557, 558) Ephraim professes to give a few short quotations from Bardesanes, which appear to be in the five-syllable metre[2]. But since Sozomen and Theodoret speak of Harmonius, the son of Bardesanes, as a writer of hymns, it has been supposed by Hort that Ephraim may have fallen into the mistake of ascribing the works of the son to his more celebrated father. The Poem now under discussion contains nothing, so far as I am able to see, which might not

---

[1] *Corpus Haeresiologicum*, ed. Oehler, vol. ii. pt. ii. p. 144.

[2] Macke, in the *Theologische Quartalschrift* for 1874, p. 51, endeavours to prove that one of the citations in question, consisting of two lines, is in the six-syllable metre; but to me this seems very doubtful. There is however no reason to assume that the five-syllable metre was the only one used by Bardesanes, for Ephraim (Roman ed. vol. ii. p. 554) expressly describes him as having introduced "measures" (ܪ̈ܚܝܢܐ), and it is by no means impossible that all these citations are taken from the same poem.

be attributed with equal probability to either. With regard to the important question of the *date*, Nöldeke has remarked that the mention of the "Parthians" (couplet 38 *a*), as the ruling race in. the East, decidedly favours the hypothesis that the piece was composed before the overthrow of the Parthian dynasty in A.D. 224; he also observes that the allusion to Maishān as a great centre of trade (couplets 18, 70) points in the same direction.

Whatever may be the ultimate verdict of scholars as to the exact date and authorship of this composition, it will always deserve careful study on account of the light which it throws upon one of the most remarkable phases in the religious history of mankind. Gnosticism is here displayed to us not as it appeared to its enemies, not as a tissue of fantastic speculations, but as it was in reality, at least to some of its adherents, a new religion. Though the religious conceptions of the author are, in some respects, very closely akin to those of the early Christians, he nowhere refers directly to the New Testament, nor does he even allude to the historical facts on which Christianity is founded[1]. Yet he does not speak doubtfully, as one feeling after truth; his convictions, such as they are, respecting the realities of the unseen world, rest upon what he believes to be a direct revelation, symbolised by the living letter "which the King sealed with his right hand." Until this state of mind is understood, the nature of Oriental Gnosticism and of the struggle which it long maintained, against Paganism on the one side and traditional Christianity on the other, must remain a mystery.

## The Metre.

At the first appearance of the Poem Nöldeke remarked that it was written in verses containing, as a rule, six syllables each. This is undoubtedly the case; but no one, so far as I am aware, has hitherto pointed out that the verses are arranged in *couplets*. A glance at the English translation will show that, while the first line of a couplet is often closely connected in sense with what follows, there is always a pause, though sometimes a slight pause

---

[1] See the very interesting remarks on this subject by Harnack, *Die Chronologie der altchristlichen Litteratur bis Eusebius* vol. i. p. 546.

only, at the end of each second line. The only passages in which this arrangement appears to be abandoned are couplets 25, 68 and 71. The first of these passages is admittedly unintelligible; in the second, sense can be obtained only by altering the text. Accordingly Wright proposes to read ܪܚܠܝ (for ܚܠܝ); but the assumption of a lacuna suffices to account for the syntactical difficulty.

With regard to the number of syllables in each line, it is impossible, in consequence of the uncertainty of the text, to give accurate statistics. Moreover Syriac verse-writers allow themselves great license in the insertion and suppression of vowels. But it will be found, on inspection, that in this Poem about 70 per cent. of the lines consist of 6 syllables or, at least, may be made to consist of 6 syllables by assuming some ordinary license[1]. In a considerable number of cases (about 18 per cent.) a line seems to consist of 7 syllables, and in some others (about 9 per cent.) of 5. By assuming *unusual* licenses of pronunciation the list of exceptions may, of course, be reduced, but even then some cases remain in which the normal number of 6 syllables cannot be obtained without some change of the text, although there is no other sign of corruption—see 18 *b*, 24 *b*, 27 *b*, 31 *b*, 35 *b*, 49 *b*, 76 *a*, 84 *a*, 86 *b*, 95 *b* (7 syllables) and 21 *a*, 24 *a*, 29 *a*, 47 *a*, 54 *a*, 79 *a*, 81 *b*, 89 *a*, 100 *a* (5 syllables). It will be observed that where there is one syllable too many the line is generally the second in the couplet, where there is one syllable too few the line is generally the first. The only lines which, at first sight, seem to have 8 syllables are 67 *a* and 104 *b*; one line (77 *a*) seems to have only 4. It is therefore possible that the poet was guided rather by his ear than by a strict metrical rule in determining the exact length of each half of a couplet.

---

[1] By an ordinary license I mean, for example, the shortening of *a'īrĕthan* to *'irĕthan* (65 *a*), of *ennŏn* to *nŏn* (80 *a*), and the lengthening of *madhnĕḥā* to *madhenĕḥā* (3 *a*), of *rēshim* to *arĕshim* (55 *a*), etc.

# TEXT

(*Asterisks indicate a supposed lacuna.*)

1 ܟܕ ܐܢܐ ܫܒܪ ܝܠܘܕ

ܘܥܡܪ ܒܡܠܟܘܬܝ ܒܝܬ ܐܒܝ

2 ܘܒܥܘܬܪܐ ܘܒܦܐܝܘ̈ܬܐ

ܕܡܪ̈ܒܝܢܝ ܡܢܝܚ ܗ̇ܘܝܬ

3 ܡܢ ܡܕܢܚܐ ܡܒܝܬܢ

ܙܘ̇ܕܘ ܐܒ̈ܗܝ ܫܕܪܘܢܝ

4 ܘܡܢ ܥܘܬܪܐ ܕܒܝܬ ܓܙܢ

ܐܣܓܝ ܛܥܢܘ ܠܝ ܡܘܒܠܐ

5 ܣܓܝܐܐ ܗܘ ܘܩܠܝܠܐ

ܕܐܢܐ ܠܚܘܕܝ ܐܫܩܘܠܝܗ̇

6 ܕܗܒܐ ܗܘ ܕܒܝܬ ܥܠ̈ܝܐ

ܘܣܐܡܐ ܕܓܙܟ ܪܒܬܐ

7 ܘܡܪ̈ܓܢܝ ܗܢܕܘ

ܘܦܬ̈ܟܬܐ ܕܡܢ ܒܝܬ ܩܫܢ

*(In the Translation, dots indicate that the Syriac text is corrupt or unintelligible.)*

1  When I was a little child,

And dwelling in my kingdom in my Father's house,

2  And in the wealth and the glories

Of my nurturers had my pleasure,

3  From the East, our home,

My parents, having equipped me, sent me forth.

4  And of the wealth of our treasury

They had already tied up for me a load,

5  Large it was, yet light,

So that I might bear it unaided—

6  Gold of . . . .

And silver of Gazzak the great,

7  And rubies of India,

And agates (?) from the land of Ḳushān (?),

8 ⌝ܘܚܡܫܘܢܝ⌜ ܒܐܕܡܘܣ

ܕܠܦܪܙܠܐ ܗܘ ܫܚܩܐ

9 ܘܐܫܠܚܘܢܝ ⌝ܠܗܝܬܐ⌜

ܕܒܚܘܒܗܘܢ ܥܒܕܘܗ̇ ܠܝ

10 ܘܠܛܘܓܝ ܕܙܚܘܪܝܬܐ

ܕܥܠ ܩܘܡܬܝ ܡܡܫܚ ܗܘܐ

11 ܘܥܒܕܘ ܥܡܝ ܚܘܪܡܢܐ

ܘܟܬܒܘܗܝ ܒܠܒܝ ܕܠܐ ܢܬܛܥܐ

12 ܘܐܢ ܬܚܘܬ ܠܡܨܪܝܢ

⌝ܘܬܝܬܝܗ̇⌜ ܠܡܪܓܢܝܬܐ ܚܕܐ.

13 ܗ̇ܝ ܕܐܝܬܝܗ̇ ܒܓܘ ܝܡܐ

ܚܕܪ̈ܘܗܝ ܕܚܘܝܐ ܫܪܘܩܐ

14 ܬܠܒܫܝܗ̇ ܠܗܝܬܟ

ܘܠܛܘܓܟ ܕܥܠܝܗ̇ ܡܢܝܚ

15 ܘܥܡ ܐܚܘܟ ܬܪܝܢܢ

⌝ܝܪܘܬ⌜ ܒܡܠܟܘܬܢ ܬܗܘܐ

16 ⌝ܢܦܩܬ⌜ ܡܕܢܚܐ ܢܚܬܬ

ܥܡ ܫܒܝ ܬܪ̈ܝܢ ܦܪ̈ܘܩܝܢ

8[a] MS ܘܚܡܫܘܢ 9[a] MS ܠܗܘܬܐ

12[b] MS ܘܬܝܬܝܢܗ̇ 15[b] MS ܝܪܘܬܢ

16[a] MS ܢܦܩܬ

8   And they girded me with adamant

    Which can crush iron.

9   And they took off from me the bright robe,

    Which in their love they had wrought for me,

10  And my purple toga,

    Which was measured (and) woven to my stature.

11  And they made a compact with me,

    And wrote it in my heart that it should not be forgotten:

12  "If thou goest down into Egypt,

    And bringest the one pearl,

13  Which is in the midst of the sea

    Hard by the loud-breathing serpent,

14  (Then) shalt thou put on thy bright robe

    And thy toga, which is laid over it,

15  And with thy Brother, our next in rank,

    Thou shalt be heir in our kingdom."

16  I quitted the East (and) went down,

    There being with me two messengers,

2 *

ܕܐܘܪܚܐ ܕܚܝܠܐ ܘܥܛܠܐ 17
ܘܐܢܐ ܥܒܪ ܐܢܐ ܠܡܪܕܝܗ̇
ܥܒܪܬ ܬܚܘ̈ܡܝ ܡܝܫܢ 18
ܓܘܒܐ ܕܬܓܪ̈ܐ ܡܕܢܚܝܐ
ܘܡܛܝܬ ܠܐܪܥ ܒܒܠ 19
ܘܥܠܬ ܒܫܘܪ̈ܝܗ̇ ܕܣܪܒܘܓ
ܢܚܬܬ ܠܝ ܠܓܘ ܡܨܪܝܢ 20
ܘܡ̈ܠܘܝܝ ܡܢܝ ܦܪܩܘ
ܪܗܛܬ ܠܘܬ ܚܘܝܐ 21
ܚܕܪ̈ܘܗܝ ܕܐܒܣܢܗ ܫܪܝܬ
ܥܕ ܢܢܘܡ ܘܥܕ ܢܕܡܟ 22
ܘܡܢܗ ܠܡܪܓܢܝܬܝ ܐܚܛܘܦܝܗ̇
ܘܝܚܝܕ ܗܘܝܬ ܡܢܘܟܪ ܗܘܝܬ 23
ܠܒ̈ܢܝ ܐܣܟܡܝ ܢܘܟܪܝ ܗܘܝܬ
ܠܒܪ ܓܢܣܝ ܒܪ ܚܐܪ̈ܐ 24
ܡܢ ܡ̈ܕܢܚܝܐ ܬܡܢ ܚܙܝܬ
ܛܠܝܐ ܦܐܝܐ ܚܣܝܕܐ 25
ܒܪ ܡ̈ܫܝܚܐ * * *
* * * * 26
* * ܘܠܝ ܐܬܐ ܘܢܩܦ
ܘܥܒܕܬܗ ܒܪ ܚܒܝܢܝ 27
ܚܒܪܐ ܕܐܬܓܘܪܬܝ ܠܗ ܫܘܬܦܬ

17 For the way was dangerous and difficult,

And I was very young to tread it.

18 I passed the borders of Maishān,

The meeting-place of the merchants of the East,

19 And I reached the land of Babel·

And entered the walls of ....

20 I went down into Egypt,

And my companions parted from me.

21 1 betook me straight to the serpent,

Hard by his dwelling I abode,

22 (Waiting) till he should slumber and sleep,

And I could take my pearl from him.

23 And when I was single and alone,

A stranger to those with whom I dwelt,

24 One of my race, a free-born man,

From among the Easterns, I beheld there—

25 A youth fair and well favoured

. . . .   *   *   *

26 *   *   *   *.

*   *   and he came and attached himself to me.

27 And I made him my intimate,

A comrade with whom I shared my merchandise.

ܙܗܪܬܗܝ ܡܢ ܡܨܪ̈ܝܐ 28

ܘܡܢ ܢܩܦܘܬܗܘܢ ܕܛܢ̈ܦܐ

ܘܐܟܢ ܠܒܘܫܗܘܢ ܠܒܫܬ 29

ܕܠܐ ܢܚܣܕܘܢܝ ܕܡܢ ܠܒܪ ܐܬܝܬ

ܕܐܣܒܗ̇ ܠܡܪܓܢܝܬܐ 30

ܘܢܥܝܪܘܢܝܗܝ ܠܚܘܝܐ ܥܠܝ

ܘܒܐܝܕܐ ܡܢ ܥ̈ܠܠܬܐ 31

ܪܓܫܘ ܒܝ ܕܠܐ ܗ̇ܘܝܬ ܒܪ ܡܬܗܘܢ

ܘܚܠܛܘ ܥܡܝ ܒܢ̈ܟܠܝܗܘܢ 32

ܐܦ ܐܛܥܡܘܢܝ ܡܐܟܘܠܬܗܘܢ

ܛܥܝܬ ܕܒܪ ܡ̈ܠܟܐ ܐܢܐ 33

ܘܦܠܚܬ ܠܡܠܟܐ ܕܠܗܘܢ

ܘܛܥܝܬܗ̇ ܠܡܪܓܢܝܬܐ 34

ܕܥܠܝܗ̇ ܐܒ̈ܗܝ ܫܕܪܘܢܝ

ܘܒܝܘܩܪܐ ܕܠܘ̈ܚܨܝܗܘܢ 35

ܫ̈ܟܒܬ ܒܫܢܬܐ ܥܡܝܩܬܐ

ܘܗܠܝܢ ܟܠܗܝܢ ܕܓܕܫܢܝ 36

ܐܒ̈ܗܝ ܪܓܫܘ ܘܚܫܘ ܥܠܝ

ܘܐܬܥܒܪ ܒܡܠܟܘܬܢ 37

ܕܟܠܢܫ ܠܬܪܥܢ ܢܬܦܢܐ

ܡ̈ܠܟܐ ܘܪ̈ܫܐ ܕܦܪܬܘ 38

ܘܟܠ ܪ̈ܘܪܒܢܐ ܕܡܕܢܚܐ

28  I warned him against the Egyptians

And against consorting with the unclean;

29  And I put on a garb like theirs,

Lest they should insult (?) me because I had come from afar,

30  To take away the pearl,

And (lest) they should arouse the serpent against me.

31  But in some way or other

They perceived that I was not their countryman;

32  So they dealt with me treacherously,

Moreover they gave me their food to eat.

33  I forgot that I was a son of kings,

And I served their king;

34  And I forgot the pearl,

For which my parents had sent me,

35  And by reason of the burden of their . . .

I lay in a deep sleep.

36  But all these things that befel me

My parents perceived and were grieved for me;

37  And a proclamation was made in our kingdom,

That all should speed to our gate,

38  Kings and princes of Parthia

And all the nobles of the East.

39 ܘܦܛܪܘ ܟܠ ܐܦܪܝܣܢܐ
ܕܐܝܟܐ ܒܡܨܪܝܢ ܠܐ ܐܫܬܒܩ

40 ܘܟܬܒܘ ܠܝ ܐܓܪܬܐ
ܘܟܠ ⌜ܪܒ⌝ ܫܡܗ ܒܗ̇ ܐܪܫܡ

41 ܡܢ ܐܒܘܟ ܡܠܟ ܡ̈ܠܟܐ
ܘܐܡܟ ܐܚܝܕܬ ܡܕܢܚܐ

42 ܘܡܢ ܐܚܘܟ ܬܪܝܢܢ
ܠܟ ܒܪܢ ܕܒܡܨܪܝܢ ܫܠܡ

43 ⌜ܥܘܪ⌝ ܘܩܘܡ ܡܢ ܫܢܬܟ
ܘܡ̈ܠܐ ܕܐܓܪܬܢ ܫܡܥ

44 ܐܬܕܟܪ ܕܒܪ ܡ̈ܠܟܐ ܐܢܬ
ܚܙܝ ܥܒܕܘܬܐ ܠܡܢ ܦܠܚܬ

45 ܥܗܕܝܗ̇ ܠܡܪܓܢܝܬܐ
ܕܥܠܝܗ̇ ܠܡܨܪܝܢ ܐܫܬܕܪܬ

46 ܐܬܕܟܪܝܗ̇ ܠܢܚܬܟ
ܘܠܒܘܫܟ ܓܐܝܐ ܕܟܪ

47 ܕܬܠܒܫ ܘܬܬܥܛܦ
ܕܒܣܦܪ ܓܢ̈ܒܪܐ ܫܡܟ ܐܬܩܪܝ

48 ܘܥܡ ܐܚܘܟ ܡܕܒܪܢܢ
ܥܡܗ ܒܡܠܟܘܬܢ ܬܗܘܐ

40b MS ܪܘܪ̈ܒܢܐ 43a MS ܥܪ

39 So they wove a plan on my behalf,

That I might not be left in Egypt,

40 And they wrote to me a letter,

And every noble signed his name thereto:

41 "From thy Father, the King of kings,

And thy Mother, the mistress of the East,

42 And from thy Brother, our next in rank,

To thee our son, who art in Egypt, greeting!

43 Up and arise from thy sleep,

And listen to the words of our letter!

44 Call to mind that thou art a son of kings!

See the slavery—whom thou servest!

45 Remember the pearl

For which thou didst speed to Egypt!

46 Think of thy bright robe,

And remember thy glorious toga,

47 Which thou shalt put on as thine adornment,

When thy name hath been read out in the list of the valiant,

48 And with thy Brother, our . . .

Thou shalt be . . . in our kingdom."

ܘܐܓܪܬܝ ܐܓܪܬܐ ܗ̇ܝ
ܕܡܠܟܐ ܒܝܡܝܢܗ ܚܬܡܗ̇
ܡܢ ܒ̈ܝܫܐ ܒ̈ܢܝ ܒܒܠ
ܘܕ̈ܘܝܐ ܡܪ̈ܘܕܐ ܕܠܒܪܢܛܘܣ
ܦܪܚܬ ܒܕܡܘܬ ܢܫܪܐ
ܡܠܟܐ ܕܟܠܗ̇ ܦܪܚܬܐ
ܦܪܚܬ ܘܢܚܬܬ ܠܘܬܝ
ܘܟܠܗ̇ ܗܘ̣ܬ ܠܗ̇ ܡܠܬܐ
ܠܩܠܗ̇ ܘܠܩܠ ܪܓܫܗ̇
ܢܥܪܬ ܘܩܡܬ ܡܢ ܫܢܬܝ
ܫܩܠܬܗ̇ ܘܢܫܩܬܗ̇
ܘܫܪܝܬ ܐܢܐ ⌜ܠܚܬܡܗ̇⌝ ܩܪܝܬ
ܘܥܠ ܗܘ ܕܒܠܒܝ ܪܫܝܡ
ܡ̈ܠܝ ܕܐܓܪܬܝ ܐܬܟܬܒ̇
ܥܗܕܬ ܕܒܪ ܡ̈ܠܟܐ ܐܢܐ
ܘܚܐܪܘܬܝ ܒܥܬܗ̇ ܓܢܣܐ
ܥܗܕܬ ܠܡܪܓܢܝܬܐ
ܕܥܠܝܗ̇ ܠܡܨܪܝܢ ܐܫܬܕܪܬ
ܘܫܪܝܬ ܡܚܪܫܘ. ܐܢܐ ܠܗ
ܠܚܘܝܐ ܕܡܫܠܝܐ ܘܡܫܥܝܐ

52b ܠܗ̇ (sic) MS 54b MS ܠܚܬܗ̇

49 And my letter (was) a letter

Which the King sealed with his right hand,

50 (To keep it) from the wicked ones, the children of Babel,

And from the savage demons of . . .

51 It flew in the likeness of an eagle,

The king of all birds;

52 It flew and alighted beside me,

And became all speech.

53 At its voice and the sound of its rustling,

I started and arose from my sleep.

54 I took it up and kissed it,

And loosed its seal (?), (and) read;

55 And according to what was traced on my heart

Were the words of my letter written.

56 I remembered that I was a son of kings,

And my free soul longed for its natural state.

57 I remembered the pearl,

For which I had been sent to Egypt,

58 And I began to charm him,

The terrible loud-breathing serpent.

ܐܫܢܬܗ ܘܐܫܟܒܬܗ 59
ܕܫܡ ܐܒܝ ⌈ܥܠܘܗܝ ܐܢܐ⌉ ܐܬܕܟܪܬ

ܘܫܡܗ ܕܬܪܝܢ 60
ܘܕܐܡܢ ܡܠܟܬ ܡܕܢܚܐ

ܘܚܛܦܬܗ ܠܡܪܓܢܝܬܐ 61
ܘܗܦܟܬ ܕܐܦܢܐ ܠܒܝܬ ܐܒܝ

ܘܠܒܘܫܗܘܢ ܨܐܐ ܘܛܡܐܐ 62
ܫܠܚܬ ܘܫܒܩܬܗ ܒܐܪܥܗܘܢ

ܘܬܪܨܬܗ ܠܡܪܕܝܬܝ ⌈ܕܐܬܐ⌉ 63
ܠܢܘܗܪܐ ܕܒܝܬܢ ܡܕܢܚܐ

ܘܠܐܓܪܬܝ ܡܥܝܪܢܝܬܝ 64
ܩܕܡܝ ܒܐܘܪܚܐ ܐܫܟܚܬ

ܘܐܝܟ ܕܒܩܠܗ ⌈ܐܥܝܪܬܢܝ⌉ 65
ܬܘܒ ܒܢܘܗܪܗ ܠܝ ܡܕܒܪܐ

⌈ܕܫܪܝܐ⌉ ܒܫܠܝܘܢ 66
ܩܕܡܝ ܒܚܘܪܗ ܡܦܪܓܐ

ܘܒܚܠܗ ܘܒܡܕܒܪܢܘܬܗ 67
ܬܘܒܡ ܪܗܒܘܬܢܝ ܡܠܒܒܐ

59[b] MS ܐܢܐ ܥܠܘܗܝ

63[a] MS ܕܬܐܬܐ

65[a] MS ܐܥܝܪܬܢ

66[a] MS orig. ܕܫܝܪܝܐ

59 I hushed him to sleep and lulled him into slumber,

For my Father's name I named over him,

60 And the name of our next in rank,

And of my Mother, the queen of the East;

61 And I snatched away the pearl,

And turned to go back to my Father's house.

62 And their filthy and unclean garb

I stripped off, and left it in their country,

63 And I took my way straight to come

To the light of our home, the East.

64 And my letter, my awakener,

I found before me on the road,

65 And as with its voice it had awakened me.

(So) too with its light it was leading me

66 . . . . . . . . . . .

Shone before me with its form,

67 And with its voice and its guidance

It also encouraged me to speed,

* * * * 68

⌜ܘܒܣܘܟܗ⌝ ܢܓܕ ܠܝ

ܢܦܩܬ ܒܪܓܬܗ ܠܣܪܒܘܓ 69

ܫܒܩܬ ܠܒܒܠ ܠܣܡܠܝ

ܘܡܛܝܬ ܠܡܝܫܢ ܪܒܬܐ 70

ܠܠܡܐܢܗܘܢ ܕܬܓܪܐ

ܕܟܒܝܪܗ ܕܝܡܐ ܬܚܘܡܐ 71

* * * *

⌜ܘܠܒܘܫܝ⌝ ܕܫܠܚܬ ܗܘܝܬ 72

ܘܠܛܘܒ ⌜ܕܥܡܗ⌝ ܡܟܪܟܐ

ܡܢ ⌜ܪ̈ܡܬܐ ܕܗܘܪܩܢ⌝ 73

ܠܬܡܢ ܐܝ̈ܬܝܘ ܫܕܪܘܗܝ

ܒܐܝܕܐ ܕܓܙ̈ܒܪܝܗܘܢ 74

ܕܫܪ̈ܝܪܗܘܢ ܥܠܝܗ ܡܗܝܡܢܝܢ

ܘܕܠܐ ܥܗܕ ܗܘܝܬ ܠܫܘܦܪܗ 75

ܕܒܛܠܝܘܬܝ ܫܒܩܬܗ ܒܝܬ ܐܒܐ

ܡܢ ܫܠܝܐ ܕܝܢ ܐܣܬܟܠܬܗ 76

ܠܡܫܘܚܬܝ ܠܠܒܘܫܐ ⌜ܕܡܐ⌝ ܠܝ

68b MS ܘܒܣܘܟܗܿ

71a ܕܟܒܝܪܗ (*sic*)—the ܕ is quite distinct in the MS

72a MS ܘܠܒܫܬܝ marg. ܘܠܒܘܫܬܝ  72b MS ܕܒܗܿ

73a MS ܪ̈ܡܬܐ ܘܪܩܢ  76b MS ܕܡܬ

68    \*    \*    \*    \*

    And with his (?) love was drawing me on.

69   I went forth, passed by . . . . .

    I left Babel on my left hand,

70   And reached Maishān the great,

    The haven of the merchants,

71   That sitteth on the shore of the sea

    \*    \*    \*    \*

72   And my bright robe, which I had stripped off,

    And the toga wherein it was wrapped,

73   From the heights of Hyrcania (?)

    My parents sent thither,

74   By the hand of their treasurers,

    Who in their faithfulness could be trusted therewith.

75   And because I remembered not its fashion—

    For in my childhood I had left it in my Father's house—

76   On a sudden, as I faced it,

    The garment seemed to me like a mirror of myself.

3

77 ܟܠܗ ⌜ܒܟܘܠܝ⌝ ܚܙܝܬܗ

ܘܐܦ ܐܢܐ ⌜ܠܟܘܠܝ⌝ ܒܗ ܐܣܬܟܠܬ

78 ܕܬܪܝܢ ܚܢܢ ܒܦܘܪܫܢܐ

ܘܚܕ ܬܘܒ ܚܢܢ ܒܚܕܐ ܕܡܘ

79 ܘܐܦ ܠܗܘܢ ܠܓܙܒܪܐ

ܕܠܝ ܐܝܬܝܘܗܝ ܗܘܢ ܚܙܝܬ

80 ܕܬܪܝܢ ܐܢܘܢ ܚܕܐ ܕܡܘ ܗܘܘ ܐܢܘܢ

ܕܚܕ ܚܬܡ ܡܠܟܐ ܪܫܝܡ ܒܗܘܢ

81 ܕܐܝ̈ܕܘܗܝ ܕܝܗܒ ܠܝ

ܠܝܩܪܝ ܘܥܘܬܪܝ ܒܐܝ̈ܕܝܗܘܢ

82 ⌜ܠܐܣܛܠܝ⌝ ܡܨܒܬܬܐ

ܕܒܨܒܘܢܐ ܛ̈ܒܐ ܡܨܒܬܐ

83 ܒܕܗܒܐ ܘܒܒܪ̈ܘܠܐ

ܘܟܪ̈ܟܕܢܐ ܘܦܛܕ̈ܬܐ

84 ܘܣ̈ܪܕܘܢܐ ܦܪ̈ܝܫܬ ܓܘܢܐ

ܐܦ ܗܝ ܒܪܘܡܗ ܡܬܩܢܐ

85 ܘܒܟ̈ܐܦܐ ܕܐܕܡܘܣ

ܟܘܠ ܬܪ̈ܥܝܗ ܡ̈ܣܡܟܢ

86 ܘܨܠܡܗ ܕܡܠܟ ܡ̈ܠܟܐ

ܟܠܗ ܒܟܠܗ ܡܩܒܥ ܘܨܝܪ

77[a] MS ܒܟܘܠ 77[b] MS ܠܟܘܠ

82[a] MS ܠܐܣܛܘܠܝ (*sic*) the ܘ being a later addition.

77 I saw it all in my whole self,

Moreover I faced my whole self in (facing) it,

78 For we were two in distinction

And yet again one in one likeness.

79 And the treasurers also,

Who brought it to me, I saw in like manner,

80 That they were twain (yet) one likeness,

For one kingly sign was graven on them,

81 Of *his* hands that restored to me (?)

My treasure and my wealth by means of them,

82 My bright embroidered robe,

Which . . . . . . . . . with glorious colours ;

83 With gold and with beryls,

And rubies and agates (?)

84 And sardonyxes varied in colour,

It also was made ready in its home on high (?).

85 And with stones of adamant

All its seams were fastened ;

86 And the image of the King of kings

Was depicted in full all over it, .

ܘܐܝܟ ⌜ ⌝ ܟܐܦܐ ܕܣܦܝܠܐ 87
ܬܘܡ ܓܘ̈ܢܘܗܝ ܡ̈ܫܚܠܦܬܐ

ܘܚܙܝܬ ܬܘܒ ܕܟܠܗ̇ 88
ܙܘ̈ܥ ⌜ܝܕܥܬܐ⌝ ܪ̈ܦܬܡ

ܘܐܝܟ ܕܠܡܡܠܠܘ 89
ܬܘܒ ܚܙܝܬܗ̇ ܕܡܬܛܝܒܐ

ܩܠ ܢ̈ܥܡܬܗ̇ ܫܡܥܬ 90
ܕܒܡ ⌜ܡ̈ܚܬܝܬܗ̇⌝ ܡܙܪܬܡܐ

ܕܗܘ ܐܢܐ ܙܪܝܙ ܒܥܒ̈ܕܐ 91
ܕܠܗ ܪܒܝܬ ܩܕܡܘܗܝ ܕܐܒܝ

ܘܐܦ ܐܢܐ ܡܪܓܫ ܗܘܝܬ ܒܝ 92
ܕܩܘܡܬܝ ܐܝܟ ܥ̈ܡܠܘܗܝ ܪܒܝܐ

ܘܒܙܘ̈ܥܘܗܝ ܡ̈ܠܟܝܐ 93
ܟܠܗ̇ ܠܘܬܝ ܡܬܦܫܛܐ

ܘܥܠ ܐܝܕܐ ܕܡܘܗ̈ܒܢܗ̇ 94
ܡܫܬܪܗܒܐ ܐܝܟ ܕܐܫܬܠܡܗ̇

ܘܐܦ ܠܝ ܚܘܒܝ ܙܩܬ ܗܘܐ 95
ܕܐܪܗܛ ܠܐܘܪܥܗ̇ ܘܐܣܒܝܗ̇

ܘܐܬܦܫܛܬ ܘܩܒܠܬܗ̇ 96
ܒܫܘܦܪܐ ܕܓܘ̈ܢܝܗ̇ ܐܬܥܛܦܬ

87[a] MS ܘܐܦ 88[b] MS ܕܝܕܥܬܐ

90[b] MS ܡ̈ܚܬܢܝܬܗ

87  And like the sapphire-stone also
    Were its manifold hues.

88  Again I saw that all over it
    The motions of knowledge were stirring,

89  And as if to speak
    I saw it also making itself ready.

90  I heard the sound of its tones,
    Which it uttered to those who brought it down (?)

91  Saying, "I . . . . . . . .
    Whom they reared for him (?) in the presence of my father,

92  And I also perceived in myself
    That my stature was growing according to his labours."

93  And in its kingly motions
    It was spreading itself out towards me,

94  And in the hands of its givers
    It hastened that I might take it.

95  And me too my love urged on
    That I should run to meet it and receive it,

96  And I stretched forth and received it,
    With the beauty of its colours I adorned myself.

3 ★

97 ܘܠܛܠܝ ܢܨܝܚ ܨ̈ܒܥܐ

⌜ܟܠܗ ܠܟܠܗ⌝ ܐܬܥܛܦܬ

98 ܠܒܫܬ ܒܗ̇ ܘܐܬܥܠܝܬ

ܠܬܪܥ ܫܠܡܐ ܘܣܓܕܬܐ

99 ܪܟܢܬ ܪܝܫ ܘܣܓܕܬ ܠܗ

ܠܙܝܘܗ ܕܐܒܐ ⌜ܕܠܝ⌝ ܫܕܪܗ̇

100 ܕܥܒܕܬ ܠܦ̈ܘܩܕܢܘܗܝ

ܘܐܦ ܗܘ ܕܐܫܬܘܕܝ ܥܒܕ

101 ܘܒܬܪܥܐ ܕܘܡܣ̈ܪܘܗܝ

ܥܡ ܪ̈ܘܪܒܢܘܗܝ ܐܬܚܠܛܬ

102 ܕܚܕܝ ܒܝ ܘܩܒܠ ܠܝ

ܘܥܡܗ ܒܡܠܟܘܬܗ ܗܘܝܬ

103 ܘܒܩܠܐ ܕܫܘ̈ܒܚܐ

ܟܠ ܥܒ̈ܕܘܗܝ ܠܗ ܡܫܒܚܝܢ

104 ܘܐܫܬܘܕܝ ܕܠܬܪܥܐ ܬܘܒ

ܕܡܠܟ ܡ̈ܠܟܐ ܥܡܗ ܐܙܕܪܙ

105 ܘܒܩܘܪܒܢܝ ܘܒܡܪܓܢܝܬܝ

ܥܡܗ ܠܡܠܟܢ ܐܬܚܙܐ

97b MS ܟܠܗ̇ ܠܟܠܗ̇ 99b MS ܠܝ

97 And my toga of brilliant colours
    I cast around me, in its whole breadth.

98 I clothed myself therewith, and ascended
    To the gate of salutation and homage;

99 I bowed my head, and did homage
    To the Majesty of my Father who had sent it to me,

100 For I had done his commandments,
    And he too had done what he promised,

101 And at the gate of his princes
    I mingled with his nobles;

102 For he rejoiced in me and received me,
    And I was with him in his kingdom.

103 And with the voice of . . .
    All his servants glorify him.

104 And he promised that also to the gate
    Of the King of kings I should speed with him,

105 And bringing my gift and my pearl
    I should appear with him before our King.

# NOTES.

2 *b* ܣܟܝܢ lit. "caused to rest," hence "made to enjoy," cf. the use of ܢܝܚܐ "rest" for "enjoyment."

3 *a* The word ܡܬܐ "home," derived from the Assyrian *mātu* "land," occurs thrice in this poem, but is very rare in other Syriac writings.

3 *b* ܙܘܕܢܝ lit. "gave me provision (ܙܘܕܐ) for the journey."

4 *b* Wright supposed ܐܣܒܪ to be a mistake for ܐܣܒܪܘ "they took abundantly" (lit. "they made abundant"). Nöldeke suggests that ܐܣܒܪ is here the longer form of ܟܒܪ. In Syriac ܟܒܪ usually means "perhaps," but, like the Jewish Aramaic כבר, it may also mean "already," and thus sometimes corresponds in meaning to the Arabic قَد. Compare the Mandaitic כבאר or עכבאר "already" (Nöldeke, *Mandäische Grammatik* p. 202).

6 *a* If the MS reading be correct, we must render "gold of the land of the upper ones." In the Syriac translation of 1 Macc. iii. 37, vi. 1 ܐܪܥܬܐ ܥܠܝܬܐ "the upper lands" are the mountainous regions of Media and Persia, as contrasted with the low-lying plains of Babylonia. Perhaps ܒܝܬ ܥܠܝܐ may be a poetical variation of the same phrase. Nöldeke proposes to read ܒܝܬ ܓܠܝܐ "the land of the Geli"—see the *Dialogue on Fate* in Cureton's *Spicilegium Syriacum*, p. ܝܐ of the Syriac text, last line, p. 19 of the English translation. The Geli (οἱ Γῆλοι) were a people who inhabited the district now called Gīlān, on the south-western shore of the Caspian.

6 *b*   Gazzak or Ganzak, the Γάζακα of Strabo, the גַּנְזַק or
גַנְזִיךְ of the Talmud, now called *Takht-i-Sulaimān*, was a locality
in Atropatēnē (Ādharbaijān) containing a famous Zoroastrian
temple—see Nöldeke's *Tabari* (Leyden, 1879) p. 100 note 1, and
Georg Hoffmann's *Auszüge aus syrischen Akten persischer Mär-
tyrer* (Leipsic, 1880) pp. 250—253.

7 *b*   "Agates"—so Wright, cf. couplet 83 *b*. But elsewhere
the word ܪ̈ܕ̈ܗܝ seems to mean some kind of textile fabric.
On ܟܘܫ ܒܝܬ Wright remarks, "Perhaps كاشان *Kāshān*, in Persia,
N. of Ispahan. In Cureton's *Spicil. Syr.*, p. ܡܐ, the ܟ̈ܘܫܝܐ are
mentioned as a *Bactrian* tribe." Nöldeke identifies the ܟ̈ܘܫܝܐ
with the people called كوشان in Tabari (ed. De Goeje, i. 820 l. 1)
and thinks that these are here meant by the poet.

9 *a*   Instead of ܐܝܩܘܣ other parts of the poem have
ܐܝܡܘܣ (couplets 14 *a*, 46 *a*, 82 *a*)—in 72 *a* the scribe carelessly
writes ܘܐܝܡܠܐ for ܘܐܝܡܠܐ, and the correction ܘܐܝܡܠܐ
appears in the margin. In 82 *a* we find a similar correction.
Thus it would seem that everywhere ܐܝܡܘܣ is the original
form, and ܐܝܩܘܣ a scribe's emendation. This view is confirmed by the fact that ܐܝܡܘܣ, used substantivally, is peculiar
to this poem, whereas ܐܝܩܘܣ occurs elsewhere, though only
in the abstract sense of "brightness."

10 *a*   ܐܣܛܠܐ "toga" is throughout the poem construed as
a masculine noun.

12 *a*   Wright suggests that for ܘܐܢ "and if..." we should
read ܘܐܢ "saying, If..." But it is also possible that one or
more couplets have fallen out before 12 *a*, and I have therefore
retained the reading of the MS.

12 *b*   ܐܝܬܕܗܐ, for ܐܝܬܕܗܐ, is a conjecture of Nöldeke's,
accepted by Wright. The word ܡܪܓܢܝܬܐ "pearl," as Nöldeke

has observed, may have been pronounced *margĕnithā* (or *mareghnīthā*) by the poet, not *margānīthā* (as in ordinary Syriac).

13 *b*  It is unnecessary to assume, with Lipsius, that the text is here corrupt; ܪܝܫ prop. "round about" occurs again, in 21 *b*, with the vaguer sense of "near." ܡܦܘܚ "loud-breathing" (so Wright)—this use of a participial form as an epithet is very rare in Syriac (see Nöldeke's *Syrische Grammatik* § 282, second paragraph).  The verb ܦܘܚ means not only "to breathe" but also "to suck" and "to smell." Payne Smith, in his *Thesaurus* (s.v. ܦܘܚ, ܦܘܚ) translates ܡܦܘܚ ܚܘܝܐ by "serpens venenum spirans."

14 *b*  "Which is laid over it" (so Nöldeke).  Wright's translation "with which (thou art) contented" would require the insertion of ܐܝܟ, as Wright himself admits.  For the sense, cf. 72 *b*.

16 *a*  ܫܕܐ properly means "to throw away, cast forth" (in Jewish Aramaic שְׁדָא is "to shed" tears), and hence it is applied to setting an object on fire (cf. the Hebr. שִׁלַּח בָּאֵשׁ).  The meaning "to leave," which we find here, is very rare.  For the use of the reflexive form, see 37 *b*, 45 *b*.

16 *b*  ܦܪܘܢܩܐ (also written ܦܪܘܢܩܐ, *S. Ephraemi Syri Opera omnia*, Roman ed. vol. i. p. 415 D) is the Persian *parwānak* "messenger," "courier," which the Arabs have borrowed in the form فُرانِق.

18 *a*  Maishān (Gr. Μεσήνη, Arab. Maisān) is a district near the mouth of the Euphrates and Tigris.  During the Parthian supremacy Maishān formed a separate, though more or less dependent, kingdom (see Nöldeke's *Ṭabarī* p. 13, note 5).

19 *b*  No place called ܣܪܒܘܓ is known to have existed, yet the name occurs thrice in the poem (19 *b*, 50 *b*, 69 *a*).  The mention of city-walls (*shūrē*), as well as the fact that ܣܪܒܘܓ is

coupled with Maishān and Babel, makes it impossible to suppose
that the poet is alluding to some obscure village, and we are
therefore forced to assume either that he called some well-known
city by a name of his own devising, or else that the text is corrupt.
The latter hypothesis is decidedly the more probable. Nöldeke,
in 1871, suggested that we should read ܒܘܪܣܝܦ *Borsippa*, which
is graphically very plausible; but Borsippa lay immediately to
the south-west of Babylon, whereas the context here requires a
place on the way from Babylon to Egypt. Accordingly Nöldeke
is now disposed to prefer *Mabbōgh* (Syr. ܡܒܘܓ, Arab. مَنْبِج),
i.e. Hierapolis in Northern Syria. The objection, urged by Wright,
that Mabbōgh is too far to the North, does not seem to be con-
clusive, for although it was possible to travel from Babylonia to
Egypt by a more southern route, the northern route was the
easier and probably the more usual one.

21 b ܐܫܦܙܐ "dwelling" is the Persian *aspanzh* or *aspanj*
(mod. Pers. *sipanj*), which properly means "a lodging-place for
travellers." The Syriac word should probably be pronounced
*ashpazzā*.

23 b I have here adopted the interpretation of Lipsius (" den
Mitgenossen meines Aufenthalts"); Wright translates "to my
family."

25 b What ܒܪ ܡܫܚܘܬܐ means it is impossible to say. Wright
translates, though with great hesitation, "a son of oil-sellers,"
pronouncing ܒܪ ܡܫܚܘܬܐ; Lipsius, on the other hand, proposes
ܒܪ ܡܫܝܚܘܬܐ "a son of anointing" and compares the phrase בְּנֵי
הַיִּצְהָר in Zech. iv. 14. But the dislocation of the metre shows
that there is here a lacuna, and conjectures are therefore hopeless.

29 b If the MS reading be correct, ܕܠܐ ܢܒܙܚܘܢ (Pael)
would seem to mean "lest they should disgrace (insult) me." But

perhaps Nöldeke is right in reading ܢܟܪܘܢܢ (Aphel, from the root ܢܟܪ), i.e. "lest they should *recognise* me, that I…." ܐܟܪ is originally "to scrutinize," and hence in ordinary Syriac (e.g. Land, *Anecdota Syriaca* vol. i. 67 l. 20, 68 l. 1) means "to repudiate"; but in Jewish Aramaic and in the Christian Palestinian dialect it means "to recognise" (Hebr. הִכִּיר).

31 *a* Instead of ܘܒܐܢܫ̈ܐ we should expect ܘܒܐܢܫ̈ܐ ܕܗܢ (Nöldeke).

35 *a* ܠܛܘܪ̈ܦܝܗܘܢ would mean "their troubles, vexations." Nöldeke suggests ܠܬܪ̈ܘܣܝܗܘܢ "their foods," Gr. τροφαί.

40 *b* Both syntax and metre require ܪܒ (as Nöldeke emends) instead of ܪ̈ܘܪܒܐ; the mistake is easily explained by ܘܟܠ ܪ̈ܘܪܒܢ in 38 *b*.

43 *a* ܢܕ (from the root ܢܕܕ) would mean "shrink," and we are therefore justified in reading ܢܘܕ, with Nöldeke.

48 *a* A comparison with 15 *a*, 42 *a* and 60 *a* seems to prove that ܡܫܢܝܢܐ is nearly equivalent in meaning to ܬܢܝܢܐ "next in rank." The word, as Wright observes, should properly be spelt with ܠ instead of ܢ, for in the Syriac translation of Eusebius' *Theophania* (ed. Lee, Bk. ii. § 19 l. 4) we find ܡܫܠ̈ܝܢܐ, apparently meaning "rulers" or "chiefs." This term is not known to occur elsewhere, and its origin is altogether obscure.

48 *b* ܥܡܗ "with him" can hardly be right. The analogy of 15 *b* would lead us to expect ܝܪܘܬ "heir," but as this word could not easily be changed into ܥܡܗ it is perhaps more probable that the poet wrote ܥܡܘܪ "a dweller"—cf. 1 *b*.

53 *a* With ܩܠ ܪܓܫܬܗ "the sound of its rustling" (so Wright), a rendering which Lipsius regards as doubtful, compare the Pĕshīṭṭā 1 Kings xviii. 41 ܩܠܐ ܕܪܓܫܬܐ ܕܡܛܪ̈ܐ = קוֹל הֲמוֹן הַגָּשֶׁם.

54 *b*  The emendation ܡܶܢܕܪܝܫ, for the strange form ܡܢܕܪܝ, is accepted by Nöldeke.

56 *b*.  "And my free soul (lit. my freedom) longed for its natural state (lit. its nature)"—the verb ܣܢܐ, properly "to miss" something which one has lost (Arab. ﻓﻘﺪ), is here used as in Ephraim's *Carmina Nisibena* ed. Bickell p. 10 l. 9 ܪܓܝܳܐ ܩܳܠܳܐ ܟܳܡܰܗ ܐܶܕܢܰܝ "Lo mine ears long for the voice of my vine-dressers!" Wright translates "my noble birth asserted its nature."

57 *b*  The reading ܟܺܝܕܰܐܝܟܪ, as compared with ܟܺܝܠܰܐܝܟܪ in the parallel passage (45 *b*), seems to be confirmed by 34 *b*.

59 *b*  For the Ethpeel ܐܬܕܟܪ, in the sense "to mention," see the examples given in Payne Smith's *Thesaurus*.

66 *b*  The text is here quite unintelligible.

68 *a*  The first line of this couplet seems to have contained some masculine noun to which the form ܢܰܟܝ, in the second line, refers. We should therefore probably read ܘܣܘܡܒܐ with masc. suffix.

72 *b*  Since ܓܠܘܬܐ is masculine (see note on 10 *a*), we must read ܡܒܗ, with Nöldeke.

73 *a*  This line is doubtless corrupt in the MS. That *two* places should be named would be very strange, for we can hardly suppose that the poet meant to represent the "robe" as having been preserved in one locality and the "toga" in another. Thus Wright's rendering "from Rāmthā and Rĕken" presents a serious difficulty, quite apart from the fact that the two names cannot be identified. I have ventured to read ܡܢ ܪܘܡܬܐ ܕܗܩܢܝ "from the heights of Hyrcania." The Old Persian name of Hyrcania,

which occurs in an inscription of Darius I (Spiegel, *Die altper-sischen Keilinschriften* 2nd ed. p. 22), was *Warkāna*, of which the modern form *Gurgān* (Arab. *Jurjān*) is merely a phonetic corruption. It is important to observe that according to Strabo (Bk. xvi. chap. i. § 16) the Parthian kings were accustomed to spend a part of the year in Hyrcania, and the Sāsānians also appear to have had a royal residence in that district (see Nöldeke's *Ṭabarī* p. 77). Being moreover a high mountain region Hyrcania might naturally be chosen by the poet as the type of the heavenly home.

76 *a* "Faced"—both here and in 77 *b* Wright translates "received," in accordance with the use of the verb in the Pĕshīṭtā, Luke xv. 27 (ܥܠܐܘܗܝ = αὐτὸν ἀπέλαβεν). But the usual meaning of ܐܪܥ is "to face," "to go to meet" (Arab. أَقْبَلَ), and this seems to be more appropriate here, since it is not till 96 *a* that the prince actually "receives" the garment.

76 *b* Unless we assume, against all analogy, that ܠܒܘܫܐ is here construed as feminine, we have either to substitute ܕܗܘܐ for ܕܗܘܬ, or else to read ܐܬܚܙܝܬ ܠܒܘܫܐ ܕܗܘܝܬ ܠܝ "I seemed to myself like the mirror of the garment." The former alternative gives the better sense, for the idea seems to be that the robe (conceived as a rational being) was aware that the prince did not recognise it, and therefore *made itself like him.*

77 *a* Read ܟܣܝܘܗܝ, and in the next line ܠܒܫܘܗܝ, with Nöldeke.

81 *a* The construction of this clause is not clear; we should expect ܠܝ ܕܗܦܟ ܗܘܘ ܐܝܕܘܗܝ, as Nöldeke proposes to read. Or perhaps, as Wright suggests, we should substitute ܐܦܝܩ or ܐܦܩ for ܕܗܦܩ, and render "whose hands restored."

82 *b*  It is difficult to believe that ܪܚܒܡܥܡ is right here, as
the use of the same verb in 82 *a* and 82 *b* would be very awkward.
Possibly ܪܚܒܡܥܡ is a mistake for ܪܡܡܥܡ (Aphel) "shining."

83 *a*  It seems probable that here a fresh clause begins.

84 *a*  Whether ܪܣܐܪܝܡ is a mistake for ܪܣܐܪܝܡ, or
merely another pronunciation of the same word, cannot be
determined.

84 *b*  The word ܐܪ "also" presumably refers back to 6 *a*—
8 *b*, where gold, rubies, agates and adamant are mentioned as part
of the equipment of the prince.

87 *a*  Read ܝܪܐܐ for ܐܪܐ (Wright).

90 *b*  Instead of the meaningless ܚܒܕܚܡܡ Wright suggests
ܚܒܕܚܡܡ, which I suppose to be a misprint for ܚܒܕܚܡܡ.

91 *a*  This verse and the three following are extremely obscure.
In the first place, it is not clear whether the speech uttered by
the "robe" ends at 91 *b* or at 92 *b*; whichever view we adopt,
some difficulties arise. The phrase [ܪܚܒܝ ?] ܪܚܒܝ ܠܝܢ "the
active in deeds" (Wright) is very suspicious. Since ܪܚܡܡܝ
is elsewhere treated as feminine, we should expect ܚܝܢ, and
for the same reason we should expect ܪܚܠܝܡ in 92 *b*, if the
robe is still speaking.

91 *b*  Instead of ܚܠܐ Nöldeke proposes ܠܐ "whom they
reared in the presence of my father," or perhaps "for they reared
me, etc." But as the preceding words are so doubtful I have
not ventured to change the text.

92 *b*  To whom does the suffix in ܝܚܐܠܒܝ refer? Possibly
the idea may be that the "labours" performed by the prince in
Egypt produced a corresponding effect upon the robe which he
had left behind him.

93 *b*  "Spreading itself out," lit. "pouring itself." Wright translates ـهاـل by "over me," but this is scarcely favoured by the context.

99 *b*   Read ـلـ٦, with Wright.   In the last few verses of the poem the " Father" seems, at first sight, to be distinguished from the "King of kings," whereas in 41 *a* they are identical.  On the assumption that the text is correct, the only way out of the difficulty is to suppose, with Nöldeke, that in 99 *b* the "Majesty" (lit. "brightness") of the Father denotes a person distinct from the Father himself, and that the "Majesty" is the subject of the verbs in 102 *a* and 104 *a*.   In the Mandaitic writings, the very same word (*zīwā*) is applied to a particular order of heavenly beings.   Whether the "Majesty" of the Father is identical with the "next in rank," as Nöldeke suggests, seems less certain.

101 *a*   ـهمaؤaمa  "his princes" is derived, as Nöldeke has shown in his *Ṭabarī* p. 501, from the Persian *waspur* lit. "son of a house," i.e. a member of one of the seven great families (called by the Arabic historians *ahlu-l-buyūtāt*).

102 *a*   ـهـ٥  "me"—this use of ـهـ٥, though common in the Jewish Targums, is extremely rare in Syriac.   But it is not to be regarded as a mere Hebraism, for in a Palmyrene inscription (De Vogüé, *Syrie Centrale* (Paris, 1868—1877) No. 15, p. 17) we read אתי לכא ית לגינא "he brought the legions hither."

103 *a*   For ـuمaؤ٦٦, which Wright gave up as hopeless, Lipsius proposes to read ـuمaؤؤ "with the voice of *the Spirit*"; but it would be a less violent change to read ـuمaمaؤؤ "with the voice of *praise* (δόξα)."